DeLONG

TPS SURPLUS

A Beginning-to-Read Book

Getting Ready for Bed

by Mary Lindeen

DeLONG

NORWOOD HOUSE PRESS

DEAR CAREGIVER, The *Beginning to Read—Read and Discover* books provide emergent readers the opportunity to explore the world through nonfiction while building early reading skills. The text integrates both common sight words and content vocabulary. These key words are featured on lists provided at the back of the book to help your child expand his or her sight word recognition, which helps build reading fluency. The content words expand vocabulary and support comprehension.

Nonfiction text is any text that is factual. The Common Core State Standards call for an increase in the amount of informational text reading among students. The Standards aim to promote college and career readiness among students. Preparation for college and career endeavors requires proficiency in reading complex informational texts in a variety of content areas. You can help your child build a foundation by introducing nonfiction early. To further support the CCSS, you will find Reading Reinforcement activities at the back of the book that are aligned to these Standards.

Above all, the most important part of the reading experience is to have fun and enjoy it!

Sincerely,

Shannon Cannon

Shannon Cannon, Ph.D.
Literacy Consultant

Norwood House Press • P.O. Box 316598 • Chicago, Illinois 60631
For more information about Norwood House Press please visit our website at
www.norwoodhousepress.com or call 866-565-2900.
© 2016 Norwood House Press. Beginning-to-Read™ is a trademark of Norwood House Press.
All rights reserved. No part of this book may be reproduced or utilized in any form or by any
means without written permission from the publisher.

Editor: Judy Kentor Schmauss
Designer: Lindaanne Donohoe

Photo Credits:

Shutterstock, 1, 3, 6-7, 8-9, 10-11, 16, 17, 22-23, 28-29; iStock, 4-5, 12-13; Dreamstime, cover (©Dragang), 24 (©Catiamadio), 25 (©Photgrapherlondon); Phil Martin, 14-15, 18-19, 20-21, 26-27

Library of Congress Cataloging-in-Publication Data
    Lindeen, Mary.
    Getting ready for bed / by Mary Lindeen.
       pages cm. – (A beginning to read book)
    Audience: K to Grade 3.
    Summary: "Dinner is over, and now it's time to clean up, do homework, play for a while, and then have a bath. Just enough time left for a snack, brushing teeth, and a bedtime story. Good night! This title includes reading activities and a word list"– Provided by publisher.
    ISBN 978-1-59953-701-6 (library edition : alk. paper)
    ISBN 978-1-60357-786-1 (ebook)
    1. Bedtime–Juvenile literature. 2. Child rearing–Juvenile literature.
    I. Title.
    HQ784.B43L56 2015
    649'.6-dc23

2015001020

Manufactured in the United States of America in Stevens Point, Wisconsin. 275N-062015

The sun goes down.

The day is just about over.

Everyone is home.

It is time to eat.

Now we can
clean up.

You can help.

Thank you!

Will you help me take the garbage out?

Thank you!

I will help you with your homework.

Think, think, think.

You still have a little time to play.

What would you like to do?

It is time to put your things away.

We can do it together.

Now you can take your bath.

Do you like to play in the water?

Get your pajamas on.

Soon it will be time
for bed.

Do you want
a snack before
bedtime?

Milk and oranges
make a good
snack.

It is time to brush
your teeth!

His heart only grew fonder. "Listen," she whispered in the dragon's ear. "Don't be afraid. Your heart will lead the way. It will be what you wish for and beyond. Now go find it."

And so the dragon flew away to find his beloved kindred spirit.

Would you like to read a story?

We can read it together.

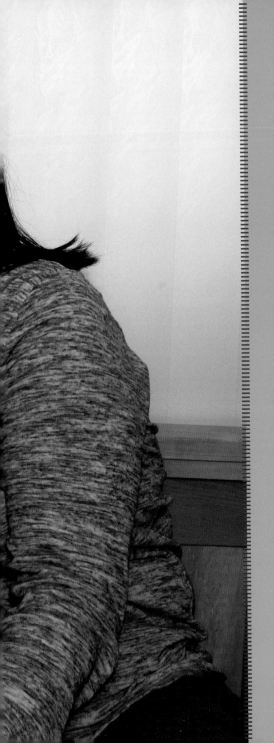

You had a busy day.

Now it is time to go to bed.

Good night!

See you in the morning!

...READING REINFORCEMENT...

CRAFT AND STRUCTURE

To check your child's understanding of this book, recreate the following diagram on a sheet of paper. Read the book with your child, and then help him or her fill in the diagram using what they learned. Work together to identify words and ideas from the book that relate to the senses.

See	Touch	Hear

Smell	Taste	Feel

VOCABULARY: Learning Content Words

Content words are words that are specific to a particular topic. All of the content words for this book can be found on page 32. Use some or all of these content words to complete one or more of the following activities:

- As you write a content word, scramble the order of the letters. Give your child a definition of the word. Have him or her use the definition and the letters to guess the word. Ask him or her to unscramble the letters to spell the word correctly.

- Have your child choose a content word and draw a picture to illustrate its meaning.

- Help your child make associations between two content words. Pick any two content words, and have your child think of something these words have in common.

- Write the content words on slips of paper. Place them in a box. Have your child pick a word and use it in a sentence.

FOUNDATIONAL SKILLS: Consonant digraphs

Consonant digraphs are two consonants that together make a single sound (for example, *ph* in *phone*). Have your child identify the consonant digraphs in each of the words below. Then help your child find the words with consonant digraphs in this book.

bath	snack	what	things
brush	teeth	together	thank

CLOSE READING OF NONFICTION TEXT

Close reading helps children comprehend text. It includes reading a text, discussing it with others, and answering questions about it. Use these questions to discuss this book with your child:

- What happens when the sun goes down?
- Why do people take the garbage out?
- What would happen if you didn't do your homework before you went to bed?
- How is your bedtime routine like the one in the book? How is it different?
- What is your idea of a healthy bedtime snack?
- What is your favorite bedtime story? Why do you like it?

FLUENCY

Fluency is the ability to read accurately with speed and expression. Help your child practice fluency by using one or more of the following activities:

- Reread this book to your child at least two times while he or she uses a finger to track each word as you read it.
- Read the first sentence aloud. Then have your child reread the sentence with you. Continue until you have finished this book.
- Ask your child to read aloud the words they know on each page of this book.(Your child will learn additional words with subsequent readings.)
- Have your child practice reading this book several times to improve accuracy, rate, and expression.

••• Word List •••

Getting Ready for Bed uses the 68 words listed below. *High-frequency* words are those words that are used most often in the English language. They are sometimes referred to as sight words because children need to learn to recognize them automatically when they read. *Content words* are any words specific to a particular topic. Regular practice reading these words will enhance your child's ability to read with greater fluency and comprehension.

High-Frequency Words

a	go	little	take	we
and	good	make	the	what
away	had	me	things	will
be	have	now	think	with
before	help	on	time	would
can	I	out	to	you
day	in	put	together	your
do	is	read	up	
for	it	see	want	
get	like	still	water	

Content Words

bath	clean	milk	play	thank
bed	eat	morning	snack	
bedtime	everyone	night	soon	
brush	garbage	oranges	story	
busy	homework	pajamas	teeth	

••• About the Author

Mary Lindeen is a writer, editor, parent, and former elementary school teacher. She has written more than 100 books for children and edited many more. She specializes in early literacy instruction and books for young readers, especially nonfiction.

••• About the Advisor

Dr. Shannon Cannon is a teacher educator in the School of Education at UC Davis, where she also earned her Ph.D. in Language, Literacy, and Culture. She serves on the clinical faculty, supervising pre-service teachers and teaching elementary methods courses in reading, effective teaching, and teacher action research.